# A Dolphin Named Destiny

By Vyana Reynolds

Illustrated by Patricia Schmidt

Published by Mermaid Tales Press

PO Box 1248, Kealakekua, Hawai'i 96750

Hardcover ISBN: 979-8-9862748-3-6
Paperback ISBN: 979-8-9862748-4-3
Ebook ISBN: 979-8-9862748-5-0

First Edition –– 2024

www.ADolphinNamedDestiny.com

**Bold lettering** is used throughout the book to suggest what syllables to emphasize while reading aloud.

# To the Wild Spinner Dolphins of Hawai'i

This book is dedicated to you, the magnificent creatures of the sea who have taught us so much about what it means to live in harmony with nature and with each other. Your grace, intelligence, and playful spirit have inspired us and raised our expectations for what it means to be human.

You have shown us that living symbiotically with nature on this planet is not only possible, but preferable — full of richness, freedom and quality time.

Your presence in the waters around Hawai'i has brought joy and wonder to countless people, and we are grateful for the opportunity to share your world.

May we always strive to protect and preserve your ocean home and gentle culture.

With Aloha in our hearts (love and respect),

## Vyana and Patricia

**Special thanks to:**
Joel Marrant, beloved editor
Adriane Wacker, art teacher and daughter-in-law
Mabel, Beatrice and Lucille Wacker, grandchildren, who love to PLAY.

**Des**tiny **dolphin lived** in the **sea**.
The **waves** were her **home**
where she **danced** wild and **free**!

Her **fam**ily of **spin**ners
all **loved** the moon**light**!
With **gold** sand be**low** them
they **swam** with de**light**!

The **sea** teemed with **life**,
they had **plenty** to **eat**.
Full-**bellied** they'd **spin**,
play play **play**! ... and then **sleep**.

Her my**ster**ious **son**ar
al**lowed** her to **see**

through the **crea**tures she **met**.
Even **you**! Even **me**!

The **fish** on the **reef**
dressed so **sparkl**y and **smart**

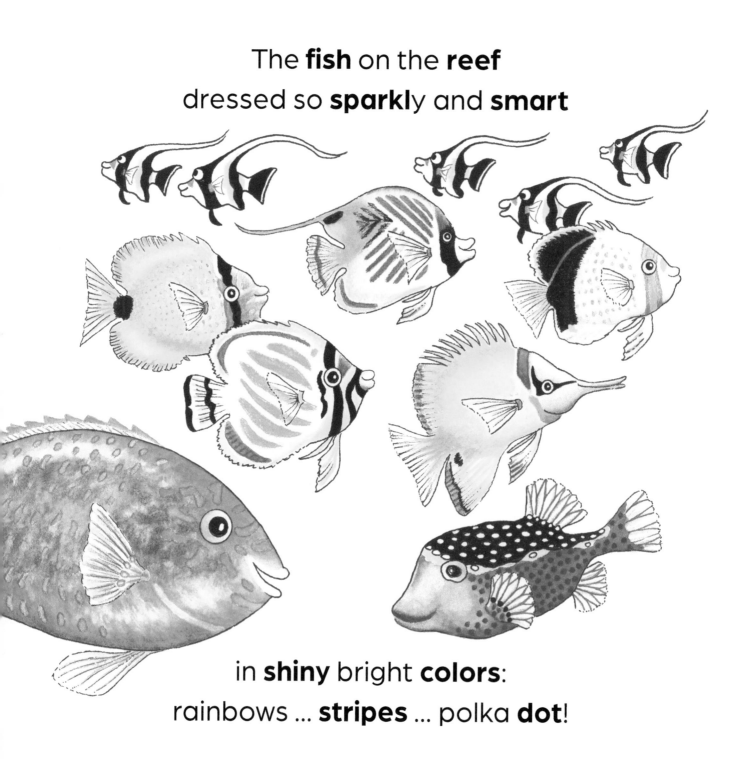

in **shiny** bright **colors**:
rainbows ... **stripes** ... polka **dot**!

One **day** she was **chat**ting
with **Humu** Von **Fizz**,

and **asked** where he **found**
fancy **out**fits like **his**.

He said **To**by the **Tai**lor
makes **clothes** just for **fun**!
With **so** many **out**fits,
why **stop** at just **one**?

So the **dol**phins got **star**ted
wearing **clothes** just for **fun**,
trying to **look** like the **fish**ies
colored **bright** as the **sun**!

She met **Ar**chie the **ur**chin,
(a **pointy** cream **puff**)
and asked, "**WHY** in the **SEA**
are you **cov**ered with **stuff**?"

"I col**lect** things I **love**
like these **shells** that I **wear**.
Do your **friends** and your **fam**ily
col**lect** things down **there**?"

"Well **no**, friend, not **real**ly,
we **just** like to **play**

passing **leaves** to each **other**
on a **sea**-shiny **day**!"

"But ... I've **al**ways liked **snor**kels
that I **spy** in the **sand**.

**Grand**pa likes **sun**glasses.
Mom thinks **pearls** are quite **grand**!

My **sis**ter, Kai**lan**i,
looks for **an**chors on **rocks**.

My **bro**ther finds **hats**.
Father's **fond** of lost **socks**."

"Well **why** not col**lect** them?"
said **Ar**chie with **glee,**
"I **love** to just **sit** here
with **stuff** stuck on **me**!"

So they **all** tried to **carry**
the **things** that they **wore**
while they'd **spin**, play, and **sleep**,
Archie **laughed** and cried, "**MORE!**"

But Octavia noticed
looking **out** from her **den**,
there was **Des**tiny **swim**ming,
but she **looked** all done **in**.

Her **friend** seemed so **tired**,
but she **swam** nonethe**less**,
"**Don't** you have a **home**
in **which** you can **rest**?"

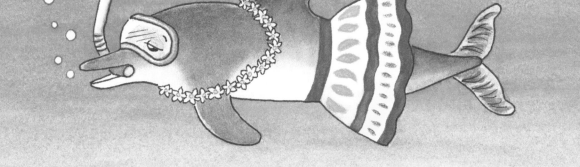

"Oh, **no**, –what's a **home**?
You know we **swim** when we **sleep**."

"It's a **place** to keep **stuff**
and store it **all** in the **deep**!"

So the **dol**phins found **homes**
in each **cran**ny and **nook**,

in the **reef** under **rocks**
and wher**ever** you **look**!

But **Ruf**us the **eel**
he **liked** to charge **rent**--
just a **game** that he **played**
wher**ever** he **went**.

So the **dolphins** got **jobs**
to **pay** the reef **rent**.

They **worked** and they **worked**
for every **penny** they **spent**.

Destiny **served** as a **maid**
ten **hours** each **day**.
With **so** much to **do**
there was **no** time to **play**!

Destiny **missed** all the **birth**days
and the **family** fun **too.**
She **missed** having **friends**.
Now **they** all worked **too!**

But **one** day she **stopped**,
asked the **big** question, "**WHY**?"

So **tir**ed and **lone**ly,
she just **want**ed to **cry**.

Then her **grand**mother **told** her,
"There were **much** better **ways**.
Just be **spin**ners a**gain**,
you'll have **hap**pier **days**!"

She **lis**tened and **pond**ered
and then **shout**ed,
"**HOORAY!**"

She **knew** what to **do**,
in her **heart**
she heard, "Play"

She **gath**ered her **family**
and **start**ed a**gain**.

With no **need** for their **homes**
They re**memb**ered that **when**...

they **didn't** need **clothes**
or to be **worki**ng all **day**.
They'd have **plen**ty of **time**
to have **fun** and just **play**!

So her **friends** and her **family**
are true **spin**ners a**gain**,
with the **great**est of **treas**ures
they be**came** what they'd **been**:

special **crea**tures to**geth**er
spin and **play** in the **sea**.
Like true **dol**phins before **them**,
they have **time** to just **BE**!

Good night.
Sweet dreams.

# Fun
## Sea Creature Facts!

Did you know that **Tropical fish make their own sunscreen** for their scales?
Find our more at www.newatlas.com/fish-sunscreen-uv-protection/37455/

Did you know that **one half of a dolphin brain rests at a time**?
Find out more at www.wikihow.com/How-Do-Dolphins-Sleep

Did you know that **octopus like to build a rock door** for their den?
Find out more at www.toucanbox.com/facts-for-kids/octopus-facts

Did you know that **dolphins play more games** than leaf games?
Find out more at www.dolphins-for-kids.com/how-do-dolphins-play

Did you know that **sea urchins collect shells to camouflage themselves**
so they look like the bottom of the ocean?
Find out more at www.marinesanctuary.org/blog/sea-wonder-purple-sea-urchin/

# How to Swim with Dolphins

Photo by Susan Knight Studios

I moved to Hawaii to swim with the wild Hawaiian spinner dolphins. First, they taught me how to play the leaf game. They would drop a leaf in front of me in the ocean and then race me to it. Whoever got there first had to perform with the leaf to make the other laugh. The dolphin would let me win the race half the time so we could take turns doing silly dances with the leaf.

I learned to communicate with the dolphins mostly through body language. If I swam toward them head-on, they would avoid me. If I swam beside them in the same direction with my tummy facing them, they would swim closer to me. They preferred it when I kept my arms tucked by my side like flippers. Dolphins also seemed to like it when I sang to them. I wonder if the sound waves from my singing are like watching a movie in their sonar brain?

The Hawaiians, some of whom have been swimming with dolphins for generations, taught me how to be "pono" around the dolphins. Pono can mean the right way to do something. The Hawaiian elders at one beach said, "Just float. Don't dive down. Don't chase." So that is what I did, but the dolphins didn't understand why I couldn't play the leaf game with them anymore.

At another beach, the elder said it was OK to play with the dolphins, but that I should notice when they were awake (both eyes open), and when they were resting (one eye closed), and "treat them accordingly." Some fishing villages never swam with dolphins at all. It seemed that each beach and each Hawaiian family had different traditions to honor, and I loved learning from their ancient wisdom.

In the year 2021, humans lost the privilege of swimming with wild spinner dolphins in Hawaii when NOAA (part of the federal government) decided it was against the law. As a mermaid, that made me feel sad since dolphins are our brothers and sisters. I was born with a terrible disability – legs! Everyone thinks I'm human, and I can hardly keep up with my dolphin friends even when I wear my prosthetic tail. See photo above.

I hope that one day, we can all learn to swim in a pono way with wild spinner dolphins of Hawai'i and the law will not be needed. Until then, we can learn how to be kinder to each other, learn to speak dolphin, and of course, play more!

Vyana

# From the Artist

I love colors and capturing the play of light and shadow in my paintings and drawings. I have always lived close to the ocean and take every chance I can to visit the beaches of my native Oregon and Hawaii, breathing in the vibrant beauty where land and ocean meet. I recognize that stories are being told in the lives we see, and strive to represent them respectfully, in both the subtle details and the real (if fancifully portrayed) connections among living things. It was a delight for me to collaborate with Vyana on the fulfillment of a life-long dream: to illustrate a children's book! I felt such joy to hear my youngest granddaughter Luci exclaim, "Grandma, this book is about PLAY!!"

I have learned so much from Destiny and her family during the year-long journey drawing and painting thirty-two pages to accompany the story about the communities within which the spinner dolphins live their remarkable lives! Along with the dolphins, Octavia the octopus, Archie the urchin, Rufus the eel, and the others have emerged from Vyana's fertile imagination to embody the amazing diversity of life— and ways of living— in the coastal waters of Hawai'i.

Every painting in our book is filled with the spirit of aloha expressing our kinship with the creatures with whom we share this planet, each species practicing its own unique pono.

May the children who read this book with their loved ones be inspired to engage our sea-dwelling sisters and brothers with ever-deepening respect and compassion!

## Patricia

Please visit me at
**www.PatriciaSchmidtArt.com**

Printed in the USA
CPSIA information can be obtained
at www.ICGtesting.com
CBHW040628080724
11110CB00001B/2

*9798986274843*